YOUR RESUME WONT GET YOU A JOB

DEVIN W. CRAIG

Table of Contents

PREPARE FOR THE GRIND It's going to be work, so get your mind right	3

The Grind	4
My Story	4
Fully Prepare yourself	6

BUILD THE FOUNDATION Resumes, linkedin, job platforms,	9
networks	9

The Resume	10
Social Media	14
Job boards	17
Networking	18
Interviews	20

WORK IT reach out, apply, follow up, follow up, follow up	28

You built it, but they WON'T come	28
You May have to find a starting or entry point	30
Chase Them Down	30

DON'T GIVE UP I Know It's Hard	32

You Can't Give UP	33
Seek out community	33
This book will become obsolete	34
Diligence and Discipline	35

PREPARE FOR THE GRIND

It's Going to be Work, So Get Your Mind Right

The Grind

Like anything else, starting a business, getting a degree, job seeking is a grind, or at least can be. And I don't mean grind in the negative sense. I just mean that it requires daily diligence, research, homework, follow up and follow through. If you let up, then like any of the other above-mentioned things, you will get less than the potential they could be. You'll get something mediocre at best.

And by the way, most of us are not professional job seekers. All of want to be gainfully employed and fulfilled at work. The last thing the grand majority of us want is to have to be looking for a job frequent enough that we get good at it. For most of us, we are not practiced at things like job hunting and therefore can use some extra support and help.

This book is meant to be that help. It's meant to be a brief companion and guide for you as the job seeker. It will most likely best serve those just coming out of college looking to start their career and mid to late career professionals that find themselves on the job market for whatever reason.

My Story

My name is Devin, as you probably saw on the cover. I'm writing this because I feel compelled to help whomever and however I can because job seeking is a huge pain point right now, one that I even experienced recently.

I found myself suddenly and unexpectedly looking for a job after 12 years of great work, no gaps, taking on increasingly more responsible roles. I was even assisted/recruited to 2 job changes in that timeframe. And then suddenly the last job I thought would be longer term and maybe even wealth building was gone before I knew it. So, there I was, after a dozen years of gainful and successful employment, I was out of a job.

To all of you out there looking for a job, I understand and I know what you're going through. It's tough, but everything will be ok.

I've been a hiring or HR manager for all of those 12 years. Doing literally thousands of interviews and meeting many people looking for jobs to take care of families, achieve personal goals and prepare for the future. I've always empathized with the people I met, but still always had to prioritize finding the right people for the team or organization. I've even coached transitioning military veterans coming out of the military going into the civilian workforce. And in doing so I've built a thorough understanding of the job market and job seeking process. But I still didn't have a full appreciation for what it was like to actually be in that position until recently.

And I'll tell you what, it was humbling, humiliating, lonely and exhausting. So, to all of you out there looking for a job, I understand and I know what you're going through. It's tough, but everything will be ok. Everything will work out.

Fully Prepare Yourself

The first thing to do is to get your mind in the right place. You'll first have to deal with why you're out of work in the first place. New out of school, lost it in layoffs, family reasons, fired? All of these have emotional effects and it's important to reflect on them and move past them in order to effectively move to the next phase.

Once you feel at peace with why you're in the position of needing a new job or career, then you can start to prepare for the search itself.

The first step in the preparation takes a realization that the job search will be comprehensive. That's why the title of this book is what it is. Because gone are the days that simply emailing a resume will do. Recruiters, HR and hiring managers are now, because of technological improvements to application processes are receiving hundreds and hundreds of applications per opening. That seems great, but it's a logistical nightmare to review all of them. That's why employers are using software programs to screen for keywords, just to help with the sheer volume. It's unfortunate for the job seeker, in one sense but totally understandable for the recruiter.

Unless you are very overqualified for the position and write your resume and application perfectly for that particular posting, then chances are you will get passed over nearly every time.

The job seeking process will require you to use a multi-pronged approach. The tools, the social media, etc, will change and even become obsolete. But this approach to job seeking will always be relevant. Here is the list of the tools that I will talk about, some are the traditional, and others are more of what are needed to be successful in the job market today:
1. *Resume*
2. *Social Media (LinkedIn and Facebook)*
3. *Job Boards (Indeed, Monster, LinkedIn, company webpages)*
4. *Networking*
5. *Interviews*
6. *Other tools (Follett Cares job resource page, company job pages)*

Once you have the tools and yourself prepared and have a presence in the right places in social media, at least on a base level, then where should you spend your time? One writer, Allison Jones, recommends the 20-20-60[1] approach to job seeking. And I believe it's pretty spot on, and I wished I would have used it with this last job search.

	JOB SEEKING APPROACH	RECOMMENDED PERCENT TO BE USED
Approach #1	Applying directly to jobs	20%
Approach #2	Getting noticed by recruiters	20%
Approach #3	Networking	60%

Ok, now let's get to work.

BUILD THE FOUNDATION

Resumes, LinkedIn, Job Platforms, Networks

The Resume

Like I mentioned in the title, the resume alone will not get you the job. If you do get a job simply by submitting a resume then you are probably overqualified. For the rest of us trying to get jobs with companies that look like they would be great to work for in capacities that we would do well in and would challenge and stretch us, then chances are the resume will on be one factor, and not even the largest. So in other words, don't spin your wheels to much about the resume. Spend a few hours on it, have a few other people look at it, then call it good.

I met with a work friend recently who had moved onto another great job and employer like I did as part of my job transition process and she mentioned that her husband paid someone to do his resume and it was beautiful. And nine months total had gone by and no new job. I don't share this story because I'm against resume writing experts or services, I think they can be incredibly helpful. I'm just saying that they in and of themselves won't get the job done. You will.

As a matter of fact, Jeff Weiner, CEO of LinkedIn, saying resumes are dead. Well great, then why build one? Well, they're not dead yet.

I've seen a lot of resumes. Maybe thousands? And they are all relatively the same. Yes, it is true that most recruiters and hiring managers only take a handful or seconds to review them. That's because all we're looking for is basic qualification. Even when I review a resume I try to be open minded about traditional qualification, but it's a ticket of entry nonetheless.

I attached my own resume right in the back as an example. Yes, this is my actual resume. The exact one I used to get my last job. As a matter of fact, (shameless plug) the recruiter, who was very experienced, told me it was one of the most unique he had ever seen. I was pretty proud of that. You see, I did it myself. It was my design. I was proud because of what was on it and how it was presented. So don't steal mine. Not because I copyrighted it or anything. Just because you need to make your resume yours.

My recommendations about resume are the following:
1. *Make it your own*
2. *Share what you're most proud of*
3. *Keep it as short and to the point as possible*

The Resume Alone Won't Get You the Job

Make It Your Own
By making it your own I mean your own words, your style, etc. My resume got me a job and probably got me skipped for some too. Which I am perfectly ok with. Because if they didn't appreciate my resume then would they may have not appreciated me if I went to work there? Did they potentially not appreciate creativity? Or originality? Well thank God because otherwise I could have been pretty miserable.

So you need to build your own flair to your own resume. A resume is a reflection of how you've spent your time professionally.

Share What You Are Most Proud of
In other words, don't just list job duties. All that tells an employer or hiring manager is what your job entailed, it doesn't tell them what you actually did with the job.

Instead of saying, "I did this or that" or "my duties were…", use action phrases to describe accomplishments, accolades, measures and impacts you made while you were there.

For example, use action words like the following to start your bullet points below your job titles in your experience/work history section:

- Built
- Grew
- Developed
- Created
- Streamlined
- Recognized for
- Promoted

And then use only the subsequent words necessary to get the point across. I also recommend using numbers and measures of your accomplishments. It gives weight and depth to your words and to each and every bullet point. Types of things you could give numbers to are profit increases, sales increases, improvement in retention numbers, doo hickeys produced, etc.

All listing job duties tells an employer is what you're your job entailed, not what you actually did with the job.

Keep It as Short as Possible
We know most all recruiters only give resumes a few seconds of review to any given resume, so don't bother making it long. Work hard to get it to one page. What's good about this is it will force you to narrow down the things you are most proud of and to word them concisely. One page is ideal. Take a look at my resume. I used every square inch. One page is more ideal with no less than 9 font and with every part of the page used, but not cluttered or junkie. The resume is for the recruiters and hiring managers not for us to feel good about ourselves so make it as easy as possible on them.

And besides, the resume was never designed to get you a job. It's actually intended to get you an interview. We will talk about interviews a little bit later.

Social Media

We all know social media is a powerful tool for all kinds of things. Promoting business, selling an idea, building community and learning. Well, as many people have already learned, it's also an outstanding place to find a job.

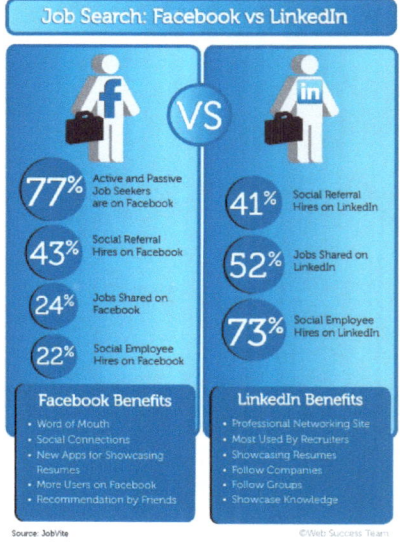

LinkedIn
LinkedIn's entire purpose is to bring economic opportunity to those in the professional world. So naturally it's a terrific platform for almost everything you need for the entire job search. LinkedIn is not only a job board with thousands of jobs from nearly every company, it's also a great place to reconnect with your network, see which of them work at the companies you'd like to apply for, research those companies, get info for the salary negotiation and even see the competition stats. Before LinkedIn all of this would have been very difficult to accomplish, but now it's all at your fingertips.

LinkedIn offers a premium service that costs $60 a month for job seekers. It allows you to do multiple to do multiple things like gives you a ranking compared to the other applicants, tells you a projected salary range for the job and tells you what skills tracked in LinkedIn other applicants. These are niceties but not necessities so I would not recommend paying for this service unless $60 a month is not a big deal for you at all.

The reason I don't recommend the paid subscription is because the only difference you get is seeing the estimated salary range, seeing your competition and a higher cap or unlimited messages to recruiters. Those all sound like great things but unfortunately, I didn't find that they worked and not only that, because it's not quite that accurate its leads to false hope or unnecessary anxiety.

This is what I mean. LinkedIn ranks you and shows you if they believe you to be in the top 10, 25 or 50 percent of comparable applicants that applied through LinkedIn. What they are using to compare you to other applicants are all of your job titles, education, certification, licenses and skills that either you listed or that other people on LinkedIn recommend or endorsed you for on LinkedIn.

The problems with this ranking system is that LinkedIn isn't the company doing the hiring. I know as a hiring manager for the past 12 years that I never ranked the way LinkedIn does. In other words, LinkedIn is using one ranking approach for all jobs and companies but each one of those companies' screens, interviews and hires differently based on different criteria and applies them in different ways. So, what I experienced was zeal when I was ranked in the top 10% and was discouraged to even apply was I was in the bottom 50%. But what happened in reality was the opposite. I got interviews with the "bottom 50%" jobs I applied for and not a peep from the "top 10%" jobs that I ranked for. What? Oh, and by the way the job I got I hardly quailed for! It was totally out of any industry I ever worked in and a type of work I've never done. But the recruiter liked my unique resume and the hiring manager wanted a people leader not a technical expert. How can you calculate that? You can't. Which is why you should never be overly confident or sell yourself short. Just humbly and confidently put yourself out there and see what happens.

If you choose not to use the premium service through LinkedIn, focus on the networking, company research and referrals, finding the people, recruiters and hiring managers within those company and use it as a job board to apply through. These features are worth their weight in gold. Often you will be able to see the person posting the job and can reach out to them directly and introduce yourself, check to make sure your application and resume went through and, if you're so bold, ask to meet them or straight up ask for the interview. You don't actually even need the messaging part of the premium service because all you have to do is send the recruiting and/or hiring manager a connection request. Just make sure to personalize it, don't just send the default message. That's pretty impersonal. Say who you are and why you're reaching out and that you would love to meet them.

And then of course apply to any and everything you would like, have some passion and hopefully qualification for and get after it!

Facebook

To be honest I have very little experience using Facebook for jobs. I did use it within the past couple years only for recruiting and it helped in that capacity.

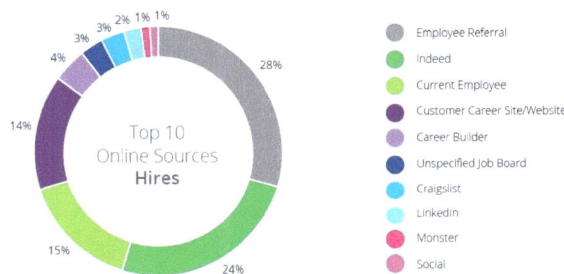

Facebook works well for localized hiring and to focuses mostly on hourly hiring for what seems to be small and medium size businesses. So if that is the type of work you're looking for, Facebook should work well. Different things you can try using Facebook is to seek out and research company Facebook pages of the places you would like to work or have applied or are considering applying to.

Although I would not recommend looking up people you are going to interview with. People tend to post more personal type things on Facebook and may be weirded out if you mention that you saw their kids or friends. So keep the research about individual people to LinkedIn.

Job Boards

Most people think this is the first place to go. I did. I started applying to jobs like crazy. As a matter of fact, I applied to 350 jobs in the first 6 weeks. It was crazy. I was so tired of typing my name, phone number, email address and job history.

But what I realized is everyone else is doing the same thing. I'm pretty sure the volume game helped me to get the dozen or so interviews within the first weeks and an offer within 2 months, but still it was grueling and not time effective. Plus, this is what I was doing full time for those several weeks. I completely understand that most people don't have that luxury.

The leading job boards have changed over the years. Right now it's Indeed. Other than LinkedIn that's where I spent most of my time. And I signed up for Indeed's email alerts from my saved job searches.

Networking

Personal Network
The reason you should spend 60% of your time reconnecting with your personal network, asking them if they know about jobs in their companies, asking who they know at their or other companies and using tools like LinkedIn to see what your extended network looks like is because nearly 60% of jobs are filled internally, as you can see in infographic number 2 based on a leading HR software company, Silk Road. Internally meaning from employee referrals or recruiting primarily and also the company's website and walk ins.

And maybe your friends and network don't know of anything at the moment but once they know you're on the hunt, they will most likely look out for you. I have friend that started his own business as a consultant but when more consulting business didn't come, he started looking back at the job market. One of the first things he did was reach out to his network and got an interview shortly after at a company one of his former colleagues now works for. I was stoked for him and kicked myself because I should have done that too sooner in my last job search. So reach out to those folks you used to work with even if you haven't kept in touch. If you enjoyed working together, they most likely would want to work with you again, so it's worth a shot.

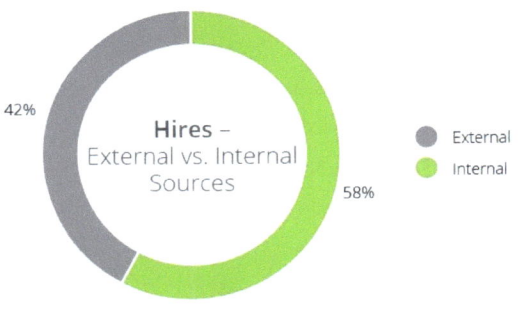

The other thing to realize is that your extended network, meaning the next level network connections beyond your first level network may have the opportunities you're looking for. If your friends and former colleagues are on the lookout for you and they hear from their own friends and network that an outside company is hiring or recruiting, then chances are good that they will point you in that direction. And then you have a lead and a name to reference when you reach out to the company.

In other words, your network, is your most powerful asset your job search, not necessarily your resume.

Company Pages

If you've narrowed down a list of companies you know you'd like to try and work for that's great. Most companies have a "Jobs" or "Career" page. And even some of them have job alerts you can sign up for and be emailed based on the criteria you select. That way you don't spend all your time just scouring job boards and company sites. Let the job alerts do that for you while you spend time and all the other parts of your job search strategy.

The other great thing about company pages is that its where you can and should do some initial vetting and research about the company. You can get a lot from LinkedIn first, and then by going through the company page you can learn more. You'll discover more about the company purpose and mission, more about its work culture and operation as a whole whether they talk about it directly or not. What I mean is that the design of the site, the wording they choose, the organization of it all speaks to how they function and what they value. For example, if the website is clean and sharp, well organized, they speak in the positive and are thorough and transparent then you could reasonably expect that they operate something other those lines. Probably not exactly but everyone nowadays knows the importance of an online presence so nearly all companies invest into it so it should reflect them overall.

Interviews

Once you're in an interview, you're pretty lucky, even though it doesn't feel that way once you're in that room. Getting to the interview means you're at least basically qualified for the job or that the recruiter or hiring manager likes your background, education or otherwise at least enough to want to talk to you. That's great news!

Most people (myself included) think *"once I get to the interview, I'm good"*. In other words, we're so awesome, people will love talking to us and automatically want to hire us. This may be true, but chances are not really.

Don't be overconfident. Make sure to prepare, but don't over prepare to the point where you come across robotic or rigid. And don't misrepresent yourself. If you do, you'll probably end up unhappy and unsuccessful and you'll be right back where you started looking for a job. Do you really want to do that so quickly and often?

We all have most likely heard the advice, "be yourself", and it's so true! I know I appreciated getting to know people and hear their stories because, first and foremost, I was genuinely inquisitive and liked people but also because I also wanted to know if I would actually enjoy working with them. We spend a lot of time with the people we work with so wouldn't we want to like them? And if we had the power, or at least influence, to choose them, wouldn't we want to choose someone that we would want to work and spend all that time with?

The interview process also says a lot about the company. Is it thorough? Are multiple people in involved? Do they have you take any kind of questionnaires or assessments? Are there multiple steps in the process? Do they give you a tour of their facility or office? How do they interact amongst themselves?

If they're thorough in the interview, with multiple steps and several people involved, then it may be safe to assume they are pretty thorough and collaborative in the operation as a whole. If they touch base regularly with you through the process, then they may be pretty focused on their employee's experience. That was definitely the case for me at Starbucks. They had the most thorough, comprehensive, professional and support interview process I've ever seen, been a part of or personally experienced and the company is unquestioningly supportive and focused on its people.

Realize that you're interviewing them just as much as they're interviewing you. Ask yourself, "could I see myself here?" and "would I enjoy it?". If the answer is no and they say no too, then great. You probably dodged a bullet.

Practice, practice, practice! The reason you need to is because we just don't interview every day. And we don't try and sell ourselves every day, unless you were in sales or something before and have an idea of what it's like. But most of us are uncomfortable selling ourselves. We can sell our kids, talk up our passions, sell a project or product but selling ourselves is tough.

Follett[3] has a great resource for interview prep and it's completely free for anyone! You can actually record yourself interviewing using questions they pose and then watch back and critique yourself. Just like football teams do. It's a little eerie, but actually quite effective for reflection. I also recommend practicing with friends, family and colleagues.

Interview Types and Strategies

There are lots of different ways company's interview people wanting a job there. The infographic below highlights the 9 most common.

Behavioral

The most common type of interview nowadays is the behavioral based. Which all that means is that the interviewers are going to try and ask you about past behaviors or stories to help predict what you would do in future similar scenarios. And most of the questions they will ask are related either to the core values of the company or based on the skills required for that particular job.

Your best strategy for these types of interviews is to:
- First, **leverage the research** you did on the company about its core values, the job you're applying for and with whom you're interviewing

- Second, start to **flush out the stories** that you think of as you go through your reflection on what you've learned about that particular company.
- Finally, **bullet point out those stories** in an easy to remember format.
    - What I would recommend is using the headers of the acronym STAR
        - *Situation* – context and background of that particular story
        - *Task* – goal that you were wanting to achieve
        - *Action* – what you did (this is where they will most likely want to hear the most detail and be careful not to use too much "we" if you were part of a team because remember the interviewers want to hear about *your* actions in past situations to predict your future behavior)
        - *Result* – and finally what ended up happening.

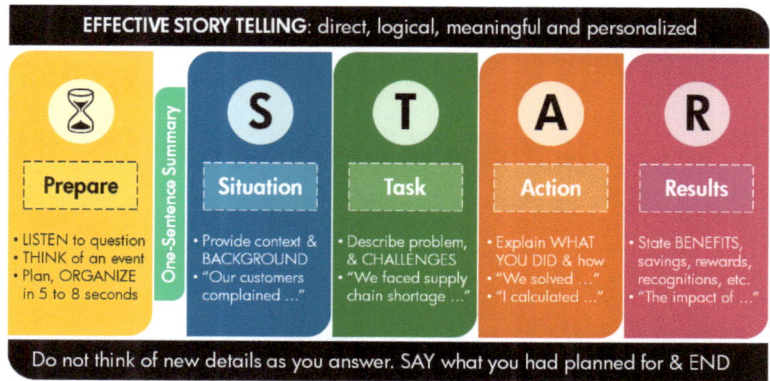

The reason I suggest using STAR is because any variation of the behavior-based interview looks for similar kinds of things.

If you have a hard time thinking of stories that relate then it may be a strong possibility you either may not be a good fit for that company or job so it may be in your best interest to move onto the next one.

> *Side Note:*
> *Not every example you share has to be a shining example of success. Often the best, most interesting stories are ones of trial and error, change and eventual triumph.*

<u>Every Other Type</u>

Honestly, the above-mentioned strategy will work for any of the other types of interviews too. The goal, like I mentioned before, is to fully learn about each other and know if the relationship will flourish. The more confident you are about what unique value you bring the more relaxed you will be. The preparation for the interview should just ultimately help you to do that.

I don't know about you, but I after I wrote my resume I felt a lot more confident. Because I got to write all the things I had accomplished and was proud of. If you've worked hard and applied yourself at your jobs then you will have plenty to talk about. Preparing for an interview is just the time to reflect on those things, which we don't normally do while at work because we're in the thick of it. And then once we complete a goal or project, we're on to the next one because that is what's expected. Use that to build your confidence and tell your story. You have much to be proud of and thankful for. Share it. If you are picked for the job after that, awesome! That means they loved you for who you are! You're lucky and you are probably going to really enjoy yourself!

One of the most memorable interviews I ever had was a panel behavior-based interview. It was with a local community college for a director level position in event and conference services. When I got to the college for the interview I was asked to wait until all the interviewers were there. 'How many were there', I thought to myself. Then a couple minutes after the scheduled start time I was walked to the room where I was going to be interviewed. I walked into the room and saw a relatively long room with nothing in it but a single chair situated in the center of a U-shaped arrangement of tables with 9 people sitting silently. That's right 9 interviewers! As I walked in I said, "wow this is intimidating", and I got a dull and awkward courtesy laugh from a few of them. I then sat down in the chair as they rigidly and formally asked me one behavioral question each. I was nervous at first, but as I started to share stories I became increasingly comfortable. At the end of the interview I asked them a handful of questions and then we called it a day. I got an email them next day inviting me to another interview but I declined because I knew I wouldn't be a great fit there.

Interviews are also great places to learn even more about the company and job by asking questions of the interviewers. Every interview I've ever done or been in the last thing that happens is that the interviewers ask 'do you have any questions for us'? If you are genuinely curious and excited about this job and company then you should have tons of questions like:
- *how do you like it here?*
- *what are the qualities of the best performers?*
- *what does a day in the life of the job or this company look like?*
- *what does success look like for this position, the team and the organization?*

No matter what style or type of interview you come up against if you know you shared who you are to the best of your ability then you should be proud no matter the outcome. Remember that chances are that you will have to do several interviews before you find the right job and company.

WORK IT

Reach Out, Apply, Follow up, Follow up, Follow up

You Built it, But They Won't Come

That's right, just because you built the social media profile, the resume, your interview skills and massaged the network does not mean that a job will come. Now the real work happens.

This is the part where it can become a grind. You're going to have to work at it, a lot. According to The Balance, it can take on average 1 month for every $10,000 in income level of job you are looking for[3]. So in other words if you're looking for a job at around $60,000 a year, it could take you around 6 months because the higher the pay for a given position, the more rare they are typically.

Don't be discouraged by this. Just prepared. Be confident that you have your foundation and just realize that it's also a numbers and strategy game. You can either go for volume of applications like I did to speed up your timeline or be very surgical and go deep with a few given companies like a different friend of mine did who got a 6-figure income job in less than 4 months, also much faster than the average.

Just because you built the social media profile, the resume, your interview skills and massaged the network does not mean that the job will come.

You May Have to Find a Starting or Entry Point

In other words, if you found a company you love and know you want to work for, they may not have the exact job you want at the time you're looking. So, you may need to take a different or even lesser paying job to at least get into the company. That's perfectly ok. As long as it works with your budget. If the money is not that critical right now this may be for the better. If you love the company and leadership, then you can work into the jobs you want. Unfortunately, a company we would all love to work for is rarer than finding a job you would love doing. A bad boss and company culture can make a great job terrible.   And the opposite is also true too.

Chase Them Down

As a hiring manager I would constantly get asked, "am I bothering you by following up with you?" I can tell you after 12 years of hiring and meeting literally thousands of people through the interview process in that time, not a single one was a pain or got on my nerves because they were "too" thorough in their follow up on their application or interview. If anything, I wished more of them would have held me accountable to making a thorough and speedy decision. It would have given me a great idea of what it would be like to work with them. That they would be someone who wouldn't let anything get in the way of their goal. That they would respectfully hold others accountable to doing their part. Unfortunately, that's rare today.

So, yes, follow up. Send a note after an interview thanking them. And in the interview ask when a good time would be to follow up. Give them a deadline if they don't freely offer it up. And then right on the day, give them a call.

If they get annoyed because you are diligent, then what will it be like once you work for them? Exactly the same. Do you want to work for someone the gets annoyed if you ask for help or follow? Probably not. Good to know up front so you can move on.

DON'T GIVE UP

I Know It's Hard

You Can't Give Up

We both know you won't because I'm sure you have other people depending on you, at the very least yourself. But it is emotionally and physically exhausting to be on a job hunt. I only had to experience for a couple months compared to the 3 – 6 months or more that many people could be looking. Just don't burn out. Pace yourself. Just know you are going to get a job. It's only a matter of time.

And just a reminder. You are a worthy. You are not just your job title, your paycheck, salary size, etc. When we're desperate or in a bad spot it's easy to be down and out on yourself. Don't be. Just because you haven't found a job yet does not mean you aren't worthy or have failed. Keep going.

Once you get a job, you'll soon forget about the time when you didn't have one or had a bad one.

Seek out community

There are a lot of people out there in the same boat you're in. Regardless if "unemployment is at an all-time low"! Well, that still means millions of Americans are looking for jobs at any given time. So if you're in that boat (and most of us will be at one point or another), then seek those people out. Find others that are currently looking or were just recently looking. There's comfort, solace and power in community.

Having a community of job seekers will at the minimum, minimize the solitude. We are social beings. We need love and connection. If you're looking for a job right now, so is someone else and there you go, commonality and community. Unite up with as many of those folks you can and share war stories, struggles, opportunities, leads, etc. The more you do, the better off you, and they, will be.

Some places you could look are Facebook, your personal network, Indeed has community boards the job seekers can post on. It doesn't matter where, but as long as it's a community that helps you and cares about you for who you are.

This Book Will Become Obsolete

Like I said above, the godfather of the professional social media world, Jeff Weiner, says that resumes will become obsolete. Well, then so will this book. Because resumes were a big portion on this book. But the point is, it will always be about you. No matter the tools, latest social media platforms, technologies, regardless of the types of work or companies of the future, you getting a job is about you finding a way to give back to society, make a contribution and provide economic means for you and your loved ones.

The point is, it will always be about you

Diligence and Discipline

In his book on success **Think and Grow Rich**[4], one of the great business and self-help classics of this past century, Napoleon Hill goes into great detail about finding success in the job hunt. And he basically boils it down to the same qualities that others whom have been incredibly successful have shown: great diligence and certainty in their quest.

Your passions, your accomplishments, the unique value you bring. Those are all worth something. They're worth a lot. You're going to help a company be even more successful. So be confident and keep up the search. It's going to require a lot of diligence and discipline on your part. Stick with it and do each of the things you know you need to each day to get the job of job hunting done.

You will find a job. Especially now that you have a great strategy, the tactics and tools you need. Good luck to you. I hope this book has helped you. Happy hunting.

References & Resources

1. The 20-20-60 approach to job hunting, Allison Jones, **https://idealistcareers.org/the-20-20-60-approach-to-job-hunting/**

2. Don't Believe These 8 Job Search Myths, Hannah Morgan **https://money.usnews.com/money/blogs/outside-voices-careers/2014/09/17/dont-believe-these-8-job-search-myths**

3. How Long Does it Take to Find a Job, Alison Coyle. **https://www.thebalance.com/how-long-does-it-take-to-find-a-job-2064245**

4. **Think and Grow Rich**, Napoleon Hill, 1937.

Infographics

1. **https://websuccessteam.com/WSTblog/2011/10/job-search-facebook-vs-linkedin/**

2. *http://careersherpa.net/employers-fill-jobs-top-sources-hire-2016/*

3. *https://www.boyden.com/media/types-of-interviews-1794111/index.html*

4. *http://www.mmcareerservices.com/career-blog/4568097217/How-to-Demonstrate-Problem-Solving-Skills-on-Your-Resume-and-At-Interview/9490592*

Resources
1. *https://follettcares.yournextstep.com/*

My Resume

DEVIN CRAIG

Community Builder

Craig Consulting Group
- Consulted a number of teams and grew their cohesiveness and overall functioning and success

JJ Rocket
- Inspired the creation of franchise purpose and values and brought them to life in all of our people systems
- Rolled out multiple franchise communication and team connection mediums that improved morale and turnover by 30% within the first year

Starbucks Coffee Company
- Field Advisor, Corporate Military Strategic Initiative
- Designed Military Connection Framework
- First Starbucks Military Community Store benefiting Goodwill's Operation Goodjobs
- 600 district team volunteer hours,

Gonzaga University
- Community Leadership Course

Target Corporation
- Nominated Community Partner of the Year for work on United Way Workplace Campaign
- Built first ever Community Crime Prevention Forum

Results Driven

JJ Rocket
- Doubled unit count and grew top line by 76% within 18 months (projected year end FY 2017)
- Improved Operating Expenses by more than a full percentage point on the P&L
- Implemented a leadership development course that dramatically improved our leadership capacity and bench level strength

Starbucks Coffee Company
- One of the strongest performing portfolio regionally in a number of business and people measures
- Improved store renovation strategy that was less disruptive and improved profitability

Target Corporation
- Double digit improved profitability in each new location and position driven by process and team improvements
- Employed district wide productivity project that improved overall labor productivity
- Improved retention and engagement with each team led

Army National Guard
- Army Achievement Medal for service to Officer Candidate School

Organization Developer

JJ Rocket
- Streamlined organizational and administrative processes that saved nearly 2% on the P&L, dramatically improved risk liability and helped make our managers and support staff's jobs much easier

Starbucks Coffee Company
- Recognized by US Recruiting Team as the recruiting district manager of the year, FY 2013
- Built Partnership model with Goodwill to help veterans
- Facilitated formation of governing team norms for district and area teams
- Promoted and recruited talent at all levels

Gonzaga University
- Communications Leadership Course, employed survey at Starbucks team to improve infrastructures

Target Corporation
- Established successful district talent assessment and development program
- Developed, promoted talent at every level
- LEADership Academy, Minneapolis, MN

PROFESSIONAL COO | JJ Rocket LLC dba Jimmy Johns | February 2016 – present
Owner and Principal | Craig Consulting Group | July 2015 - present
District Manager | Starbucks Coffee Company | May 2012 – February 2016
Executive Team Leader | Assets Protection, HR, Logistics | Target Corporation | March 2006 – May 2012
Platoon Leader | Training Assistant | Army National Guard | WA | NM | January 2001 – April 2010

ACADEMIC Master of Arts | Organizational Leadership | Gonzaga University | May 2014
Bachelor of Arts | Political Science | Minor's in Law, Religion | University of Washington | Seattle | May 2005
Associate of Arts | New Mexico Military Institute | Roswell, NM | June 2003